I0901203

MODELS OF FAITH FOR GIRLS

MODELS of Faith for Girls

STORIES AND REFLECTIONS ON Heroes for Life

TONY PICHLER & PAULA RIEDER

TWENTY-THIRD PUBLICATIONS
twentythirdpublications.com

TWENTY-THIRD PUBLICATIONS
One Montauk Avenue, Suite 200
New London, CT 06320
(860) 437-3012 or (800) 321-0411
www.twentythirdpublications.com

Images: ©Shutterstock.com; Pope Francis (pages 28, 30) M.MIGLIORATO/CPP/CIRIC

ISBN: 978-1-62785-524-2
Printed in the U.S.A.

bayard A division of Bayard, Inc.

TABLE OF CONTENTS

God has created you to be a very special person! Do you believe that?

Really believe that? But you cannot become that special person on your own. You need the help of other people, and you need the guidance of what are called virtues.

It has been pointed out that a young person needs a minimum of three important people in his or her life to grow up to be a healthy, great adult. Those three people are in addition to your parents. Who are those three or more people for you? A grandparent? An aunt or uncle? A teacher? A coach? These are people you know, respect, and look up to in life. And they know you.

Yet there are also people we can look up to in life whom we do not personally know, and they do not know us. They are our everyday heroes. These heroes may be living or deceased. The thing about these heroes is that there is something in their life that we can use as an example for our own life. Each person in this book is lifted up as a hero for you to consider. And each person is linked to a virtue.

What is a virtue? A virtue is a standard by which we live. It is the ability to act on that standard, and to live up to it. There are many virtues. Which virtues do you most hold up and follow in your life? With what hero or heroes do you most identify?

Each chapter focuses on a different everyday hero. The life of the person is discussed. Then the virtue that most fits her or his life is described. An activity is provided for you to work with the virtue. A reflection question or two is also provided to help you think about how the virtue is lived out in your own life. Finally, an action step is included to help you in living out the virtue and following in the footsteps of the everyday hero.

What hero do you most identify with in your life? Maybe one day someone will say that it is you who they want to be like! Be a hero!

Rosa Parks

I see myself as a woman of color, as an African American woman. But other people have called me the First Lady of Civil Rights and the Mother of the Freedom Movement. I was involved in the early days of the Civil Rights Movement in the 1940s and '50s, mainly working on voter registration for everyone. But then there was that one day! That day that changed my life. On December 1, 1955, I refused to give up my seat to a white person in the "colored section" on the Montgomery, Alabama, city bus. This action sparked a bus boycott by the African American community in Montgomery that lasted a year and became the first important action in the Civil Rights Movement.

I received a lot of national recognition from that one, simple action. But I also suffered too. I went to work with Martin Luther King Jr. to work toward equality for people of all races and cultures.

I died on October 24, 2005 at the age of 92. My spirit lives on, not only in people of color, but all people who take a stand (or a seat!) for what is right.

Her Virtue

FAITH

"I have faith in you!" "Oh, ye of little faith!" "Have a little faith in me." Have you ever heard these sayings? Maybe they were said of you. Maybe you used them when speaking of someone else. Whichever, faith is the virtue that requires a little leap. Sometimes a big leap! Faith is a gift from God that helps you take that leap from what you can see and touch to what you cannot see and cannot touch.

Rosa Parks was not sure what her actions would result in on that Montgomery bus. But she relied on a future that would see African American people and white people as equals. By staying seated, by taking that leap of faith, she set in motion events that would change the face of race relations in the United States for decades to come.

ACTIVITY

Faith Labyrinth: Labyrinth is a sacred path. Find your way from the start point to the center of the labyrinth, reflecting on the faith of Rosa Parks and the leap she took as refused to give up her seat.

JOURNAL / REFLECTION

Has faith ever given you the courage to stand up for something? If so, give an example.

ACTION

While sitting in a public space, take a moment to see life through the eyes of those who surround you.

HER WORDS

Each person must live their life as a model for others.

My only concern was to get home after a hard day's work.

People always say that I didn't give up my seat because I was tired, but that isn't true. I was not tired physically... No, the only tired I was, was tired of giving in.

Amelia Earhart

Do you believe I can fly? I certainly did! I was the first woman to fly solo across the Atlantic Ocean. I was determined to do it and I did! On May 20, 1932, I set out from Newfoundland, Canada, and flew across the ocean to Londonderry, Northern Ireland, where I landed the next day, on May 21. This wasn't my only record for flight, but it was probably the one that most people remember the most.

I was involved in more than just flying airplanes. I also taught at Purdue University and became an early supporter of equal rights for women. One of the things I am most proud of is that I helped to form the Ninety-Nines, an organization that supported female pilots.

In 1937 my navigator and I were attempting to fly around the world when our airplane disappeared in the Pacific Ocean. My navigator and I know what happened, but unfortunately no one else does; so our disappearance remains an unsolved mystery.

Her Virtue

HOPE

It is said that without vision, it is difficult for people to move forward. Another way to speak about vision is with the word *hope*. Hope is when you want or desire something, and you expect that, at least someday, this desire will become a reality. You might hope you will receive a new bike for Christmas. You might even expect to receive one, as you drop hints (maybe even writing a letter to Santa Claus) that the bike you really want can be found in a store at the mall. We do not always have our hopes become reality. But if we lose hope, we lose everything. Keep the flames of hope alive!

Amelia Earhart had a hope that would not die. She hoped that she had the equipment, knowledge, and the energy to fly across the ocean. She hoped that she would make it without crashing and become the first woman to do so. Her hope turned into a reality when she landed in Ireland after the long flight. She hoped that she could do it! And she *did* it!

ACTIVITY

Amelia's flight: Find the words that fit each cloud and help Amelia fly across the ocean: **dream**, **wish**, **faith**, **belief**, **goal**, **promise**.

_ _ _ _ _ _ _

_ _ _ _

_ _ _ _

_ _ _ _ _

_ _ _ _ _ _

_ _ _ _ _

HER WORDS

You can do anything you decide to do. You can act to change and control your life; and the procedure, the process, is its own reward.

I have often said that the lure of flying is the lure of beauty.

JOURNAL / REFLECTION

What is something you hope for, and how can you make that dream become a reality?

ACTION

Share your dream with someone you trust, and create the steps needed in making the above dream become a reality.

Martin Luther King Jr.

I had a dream! And though I may not have lived long enough to fully realize that dream, I did help to make great strides in the civil rights of African Americans. Beginning in 1955, while serving as a Baptist minister for a church in Montgomery, Alabama, I led the bus boycott that was inspired by Rosa Parks. Then I continued to lead the march toward civil rights until I was killed by an assassin in Memphis, Tennessee, in 1968.

I must admit that one of my favorite and most memorable moments was the March on Washington in 1963. Nearly 250,000 people, both black and white, gathered at the Lincoln Memorial on the Mall in Washington, DC. There I delivered what is still considered one of the greatest speeches of all time—my "I Have a Dream" speech.

I was humbled to receive the Nobel Peace Prize in 1964. I was assassinated in 1968 prior to my involvement in what I called the Poor People's March. Each January people celebrate and remember me on my special day.

His Virtue

LOVE

How many songs do you know that have the word "love" in them? Go ahead! Count them up! We will give you time. Ok, are you back? How many did you remember? Why are there so many songs with the word "love"? Probably because love is the foundation of all of our relationships. Think about your relationship with your parents. Or your brother or sister, if you have one. Or your best friend. What do all of these relationships have in common? Most likely, love. You love and you are loved. That is the basis of our relationship with God too. God has loved us so much that God brought us into the world and even sent his only Son, Jesus, to us over 2,000 years ago to show us how to love. Check it out in the Bible. Love is written all over it!

Martin Luther King Jr. was a man of love. He loved his family. He loved his neighbors. And he loved all people—but especially those who shared his skin color. Martin Luther King Jr. loved everyone so much that he fought for the freedom of all African Americans and dreamed of the day when everyone would love each other—black and white, rich and poor, male and female. Like Jesus, Martin Luther King Jr. loved people so much that it eventually cost him his life. How much do you love?

ACTIVITY

Using the list below, unscramble the letters in the hearts.

Care
Emotion
Friendship
Devotion
Charity
Like

dinsfipher

voditone

hiacryt

elki

acer

mootine

HIS WORDS

Darkness cannot drive out darkness; only light can do that. Hate cannot drive out hate; only love can do that.

I have a dream that my four little children will one day live in a nation where they will not be judged by the color of their skin, but by the content of their character.

Faith is taking the first step even when you don't see the whole staircase.

JOURNAL / REFLECTION

What is the person or thing that you love most in life?

ACTION

Ask a family member to tell you about their day.

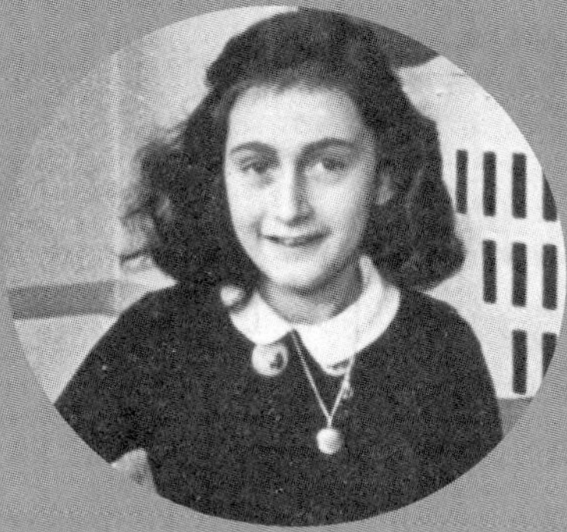

Anne Frank

Have you ever read my book, *The Diary of a Young Girl*? If not, make it a homework assignment! I was a young Jewish girl who grew up in Amsterdam, Netherlands, in the 1930s and '40s. When the Nazis came into power and controlled my home country, my family and I needed to go into hiding, finding a safe place behind a wall in my father's office. While in hiding I kept a journal, or diary, until my family and I were captured by the Nazis and placed in a concentration camp. I was killed in the death camp at the age of fifteen, during the spring of 1944. My diary was discovered by my father's secretary. *The Diary of a Young Girl* has since become a best seller, translated into sixty languages and read by millions.

In June 1999, *Time Magazine* published a special edition called: "Time 100: The Most Important People of the Century." I was honored to be one of those people.

Her Virtue

KINDNESS

Kindness just comes naturally to some people. Especially young girls and boys. It is almost as if they were wired that way. God created you to be good and kind. Check it out in the first chapter of Genesis, the first book of the Bible. Each day God creates something. And at the end of each day God sits back and reflects on the goodness and kindness that has been created. "And God saw that it was good." And the best thing is that we are created in the image and likeness of God, who happens to be all good and all kind. So we have that going for us! We just need to try to live up to that each and every day. Be kind!

Anne Frank was a kind girl. Face it—if you and your family were holed up in a room for hours, day after day would you be kind to each other? Your nerves would be shot. Your family would be tense and scared. How could you be kind to each other? Somehow Anne Frank knew exactly how to do this. She was born in the image and likeness of God, and she showed that every day of the fifteen years of her life. Can we say the same?

ACTIVITY

To open the diary, fill in the missing letters. Then unscramble the letters to use the key in finding the image and likeness of God in you.

How wo__derful it i__ that nobo__y need wait a sin__le m__ment before __tarting to impr__ve th__ world.

___ ___ ___ ___ ___ ___ ___ ___

JOURNAL / REFLECTION

Do you see the goodness in others? How does that help you to be kind?

ACTION

Make something for someone that you know they will appreciate and give it to them.

HER WORDS

Everyone has inside of them a piece of good news. The good news is that you don't know how great you can be! How much you can love! What you can accomplish! And what your potential is!

Human greatness does not lie in wealth or power, but in character and goodness. People are just people, and all people have faults and shortcomings, but all of us are born with a basic goodness.

Audrey Hepburn

I loved to act! The stage was where I found my home. Yes, you might have seen me in the movies. But it was on the stage, in front of a live audience, that I felt the energy and passion that God gifted me with since I was a little girl. I did gain a lot of recognition as an accomplished actress, both on the Broadway stage and on the Hollywood screen. I even earned a Tony Award and an Academy Award for my work, which included such films as *Breakfast at Tiffany's* and *My Fair Lady*. I loved both of those films!

Yet as I grew older, I desired to work less and less in the film and theater industry and instead focus on helping people. I became a volunteer for UNICEF, the international non-profit organization known for helping poor children in Third World countries. I loved that work! I could make a difference in these children who needed so much help. In 1992 I received the Presidential Medal of Freedom for my volunteer work. A month after receiving this wonderful award I died of cancer.

Her Virtue

GENEROSITY

That is one way to look at generosity. We are blessed with so much; especially in the United States. How well do we give away some of our things? John the Baptist tells his followers that if they have two coats they should give away one to the poor. That is generosity. Are you generous? Do you keep everything for yourself or do you give away some of what you have? Give until it hurts.

Audrey Hepburn certainly had two coats! She was a wealthy person who made a fortune through her acting career. Rather than keeping her riches all for herself, Audrey opened her heart, and her wallet, to the poor. She was known for her work with poor children in developing countries, especially through UNICEF. While Audrey could have kept her money and wealth for herself, she was generous and shared with those who needed it more. She shared her second coat!

ACTIVITY

John the Baptist said, "Whoever has two coats must share with anyone who has none." Which one of these coats is not like the others?

HER WORDS

Since the world has existed, there has been injustice. But it is one world, the more so as it becomes smaller, more accessible. There is just no question that there is more obligation that those who have should give to those who have nothing.

The beauty of a woman must be seen from in her eyes, because that is the doorway to her heart, the place where love resides.

People, even more than things, have to be restored, renewed, revived, reclaimed, and redeemed; never throw out anyone.

JOURNAL / REFLECTION

In the past, how has your generosity made you feel? How has it made a difference in the lives of those with whom you shared generously?

ACTION

Give away an extra coat or sweater to your local shelter or thrift shop.

Saint Mother Teresa

People know me as a short but generous woman of God. I was living contentedly as a Sister of Loreto and teaching schoolchildren when God touched my life and called me to serve the poorest of the poor. In 1946 I moved to Calcutta, India, and formed a community of sisters known as the Missionaries of Charity. The sisters and I served the poor who were dying of leprosy and other miserable diseases. I also served in soup kitchens, orphanages, and schools.

It was because of my work in the slums of Calcutta and around the world that I was granted the Nobel Peace Prize. I died on September 5, 1997, and was canonized a saint in 2016 by Pope Francis. I am now known as St. Teresa of Calcutta.

Her Virtue

EMPATHY

Think of a time when someone you love was sad. Were you sad with them? Did you feel their sadness in your own heart? If so, what you were feeling was empathy. When we feel someone else's pain or can identify with their hurt or pain because we have experienced the same thing ourselves—that is empathy.

St. Teresa of Calcutta was known for her empathy among the poorest of the poor in the slums of Calcutta, India. One of her most famous quotes was: "Because we cannot see Christ, we cannot express our love to him, but our neighbors we can always see, and we can do to them what, if we saw him, we would like to do to Christ." With this kind of empathy, St. Teresa felt the pain of the poor and lepers in her city and cared for them. No greater love is there than that!

ACTIVITY

In what ways have you shown empathy to those in your family, school, and community? How could you do so in the future? Complete the chart below:

SETTING	EMPATHY I HAVE SHOWN	ACTION FOR THE FUTURE
Family		
School		
Community		

JOURNAL / REFLECTION

When have you felt the pain or the joy of another person? Write about it.

ACTION

Watch the following YouTube clip:

https://www.youtube.com/watch?v=1Evwgu369Jw

HER WORDS

Loneliness and the feeling of being unwanted is the most terrible poverty.

We ourselves feel that what we are doing is just a drop in the ocean. But the ocean would be less because of that missing drop.

If you can't feed a hundred people, then feed just one.

Not all of us can do great things. But we can do small things with great love.

Pope Francis

They say that you cannot go home again! Well I did! And I loved every minute of my time there! I was born in Buenos Aires, Argentina, on December 17, 1936. I love my hometown! After some early health issues, I became a Jesuit priest in 1969. I quickly became seen as a leader in the Jesuit religious order, the group of men I lived and prayed with in community. In 1992 I was honored to be named a bishop. In 1998 I became Archbishop of Buenos Aires, my hometown. I was thrilled! I never wanted to leave there and believed that I would serve those beautiful people until my retirement and beyond. But that is not what God had in mind! On March 13, 2013, I was elected by my fellow cardinals as the 266th pope to lead the Roman Catholic Church. I took the name Francis after my model of faith, St. Francis of Assisi. You see, it is good to have a model whose example you can follow!

I find great joy in serving God's people. I hope you see that joy and peace on my face every day!

His Virtue

JOY/HUMOR

Joy and humor go together like peanut butter and chocolate. You could have one without the other, but together they taste so much better! Joy is the peace you have within you when you know who you are, why you are, and what God has created you to do in order to shine God's love in this world. Joy comes from the inside and beams out to everyone we meet. A sense of humor is something you are born with—it is God-given. Some people are born with the ability to make people laugh. Others have the ability to know when something is funny and laugh freely about that part of life.

Pope Francis always seems to have a smile on his face. The joy he experiences on the inside comes from his many years of experience in knowing that he is a child of God and that God has blessed him with incredible gifts. He freely shares this joy with others, many times through his sense of humor. How many times have you seen a frown on the face of Pope Francis? How many times have you seen a smile?

ACTIVITY

Enjoy these knock knock jokes, and then write one of your own in the space below.

Knock knock.
Who's there?
Tank.
Tank who?
You're welcome.

Knock knock.
Who's there?
Spell.
Spell who?
Okay: W-H-O.

Knock knock.
Who's there?
____
____
____

HIS WORDS

We must restore hope to young people, help the old, be open to the future, spread love. Be poor among the poor. We need to include the excluded and preach peace.

Oh, how I would like a Church that is poor and is for the poor.

I see the church as a field hospital after battle. It is useless to ask a seriously injured person if he has high cholesterol and about the level of his blood sugars. You have to heal his wounds. Then we can talk about everything else.

JOURNAL / REFLECTION

What brings you joy? Write about it.

ACTION

Find a way to bring a smile to someone you meet.

Albert Schweitzer

People have said that I was many things to many people. I was a theologian, organist, writer, philosopher, and physician. Yet, I am probably most remembered for two things: my search for the historical, human Jesus to help us balance our views of Jesus and his divinity, and my outreach to the poor of Africa. I loved the people of Africa so deeply that I founded a hospital for the poor in the African country now known as Gabon.

I was honored to receive the Nobel Peace Prize in 1952 for my writing and works of service with the poor.

When you wonder if you should do your homework or study for that test or quiz, remember me as a person who tried to use all of the gifts God gave me. Now it is your turn. Try your hardest to use your gifts and talents!

His Virtue

COMPASSION

Words are great! When you break down a word to understand its meaning, you can learn more about the word. Compassion is a great word! You know what passion is. Jesus suffered and was killed on a cross—we call this his "passion." When we say that someone fully puts themselves into a project or a game, they have "passion." The "com" that begins the word means to do something with another person. Other words that use the same "com" are companion, company, compete. We do not do things alone. We feel for each other.

As we walk through life with others we begin to feel their pain and their joy. We have passion with them.

Albert Schweitzer was a companion to many people. With his medical background he was able to suffer with the people he served. The people of Africa suffered much in the twentieth century. They had a caring and compassionate man, Albert Schweitzer, to walk beside them in their suffering.

ACTIVITY

You and Albert Schweitzer are taking a trip across Africa. Along the way you encounter many interesting animals. Name each animal using the key below.

Rhino Zebra Monkey Ostrich
Giraffe Crocodile

HIS WORDS

At times our own light goes out and is rekindled by a spark from another person. Each of us has cause to think with deep gratitude of those who have lighted the flame within us.

An optimist is a person who sees a green light everywhere, while a pessimist sees only the red stoplight...The truly wise person is color-blind.

Do something for somebody every day for which you do not get paid.

Example is leadership.

JOURNAL / REFLECTION

Who has been a friend to you as you care for others?

ACTION

Create something that will bring a smile to others and share it with them.

Ruth and Naomi

Where will you find us? Our story is told in the Bible in a book named after me: Ruth. I was the great-grandmother of King David, the great leader of Israel. I never saw him rise to power, as I was dead by the time that happened. But I was so proud of that boy! My biggest claim to fame probably comes through my relationship with Naomi, my mother-in-law.

In the Book of Ruth (you know, that one named after me!), I am the main character. I accept the God of the Israelites, and that of Naomi, my mother-in-law, as my own God. The book named after me and the stories it contains are highly regarded among the Jewish people as well as Christians. This story of faithfulness and friendship gives us a great example of how to be a friend. I hope you like it!

Their Virtue

FRIENDSHIP

That's what friends are for! Think about your best friend. What does that person do for you? What role does that person play in your life? How does this friend make you a better person? What would you do without him/her? Friends are those who love each other without reservation. They share a love and concern for each other that is not necessarily shared with everyone. Friends share a special bond of trust and respect. You know you have a true friend when that person knows you better than you even know yourself sometimes.

Ruth and Naomi were true friends. But the unique thing about their relationship is that they were related through marriage. Ruth was Naomi's daughter-in-law. This relationship, which began through Ruth's love of her late husband, was, over time, shared between friends. They could then say to each other: "Wherever you go, I will go. And where you stay, I will stay" (Ruth 1:16).

ACTIVITY

Can you find these words?

KIND
FUNNY
HONEST
CARING
GENEROUS
CHEERFUL
BELIEVABLE
GIVING
EASYGOING
CONSIDERATE

W	T	B	G	I	V	I	N	G	U	V	E
X	S	Q	E	N	W	F	T	D	I	H	A
P	E	X	J	L	L	O	X	T	D	W	S
Y	N	G	Z	J	I	P	G	F	W	X	Y
C	O	N	S	I	D	E	R	A	T	E	G
F	H	Q	G	O	N	T	V	S	M	M	O
L	U	F	R	E	E	H	C	A	G	E	I
F	X	N	R	R	N	L	K	N	B	S	N
E	K	O	N	W	K	K	I	C	Y	L	G
S	U	Y	I	Y	Y	R	N	Y	R	C	E
S	B	Q	X	A	A	V	D	F	Y	R	R
I	X	K	A	C	X	P	F	F	Y	Y	X

JOURNAL / REFLECTION

Who has been a good friend to you? Why?

ACTION

Consider performing a random act of kindness. Some examples might include:

Sit next to a person who is sitting alone in the lunchroom.

Take in your neighbor's garbage cans.

Hold the door open for someone who is walking behind you.

THEIR WORDS

Where you go I will go, and where you stay I will stay. Your people will be my people and your God my God. Where you die I will die, and there I will be buried. May the Lord deal with me, be it ever so severely, if even death separates you and me.

Yoani Sanchez

There are many ways to be a hero. I was born in Cuba at a time when it had a repressive, communist government allied with the Soviet Union. After college I moved to Switzerland to begin a new life. There I took up computer technology to provide for myself as well as give my life more meaning. Equipped with this new knowledge and skill, I returned to Cuba and started a magazine called *Contodos*. This new magazine gave people a news source—and expressions of freedom as well. I am probably best known for the development of a blog that I called Generation Y. The blog was translated into seventeen languages around the world, and through it I touched the lives of countless people.

In 2008 *Time* Magazine voted me as one of the top 100 most influential people in the world. Former U.S. President Barack Obama even wrote that my blog "provides the world a unique window into the realities of daily life in Cuba" and stated that I had helped to "empower fellow Cubans to express themselves through the use of technology."

Her Virtue

HONESTY

Quick! When is a time that you did not tell the truth? How did that hurt another person? How did that hurt yourself? Honesty is about telling the truth—about not lying. But it is more than that. Honesty is doing the right thing always, even when no one is looking. There is an old saying: "What you do in the dark will come to light." An honest person does the right thing in the darkness *and* in the light.

Yoani Sanchez is an honest person. At a young age she understood the difference between right and wrong. She used the power of technology, and her virtue of honesty, to speak powerfully to her people in Cuba and around the world. Millions of people, speaking many languages, have recognized and respected her honesty. Can you follow her lead? Let's be honest!

ACTIVITY

Decode the message using the appropriate symbols.

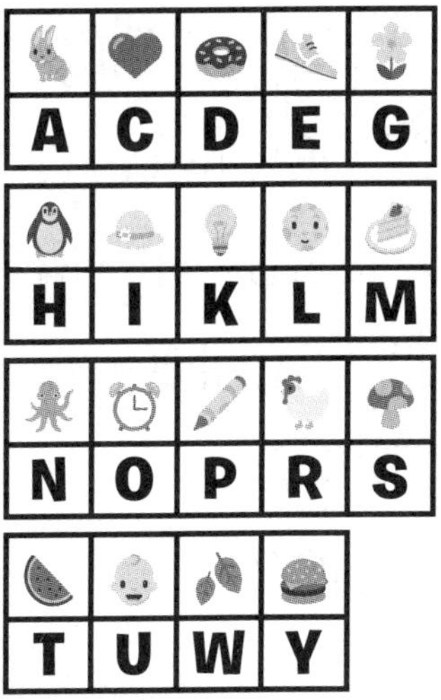

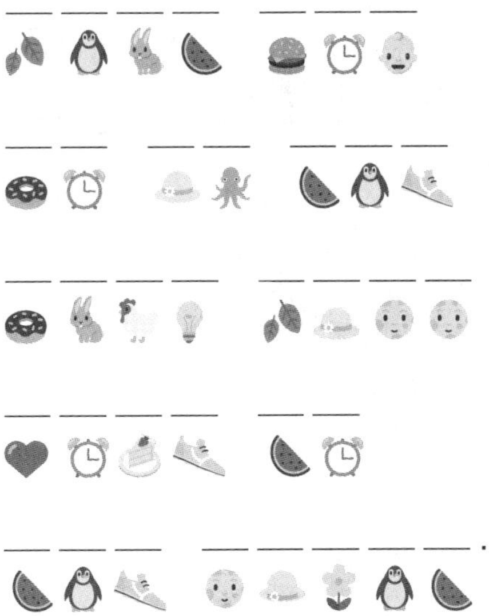

HER WORDS

Freedom is fundamentally the possibility of standing on a street corner and shouting, "There is no freedom here!"

We live turned away from the sea because it does not connect us; it encloses us. There is no movement on it. People are not allowed to buy boats because if they had boats, they would go to Florida. We are left, as one of our poets put it, with the unhappy circumstance of water at every turn.

JOURNAL / REFLECTION

When was the last time that you found it difficult to be honest? Write about it.

ACTION

Learn more about your community by reading the newspaper, listening to the news on the radio, and watching the news on your local TV station.

Helen Keller

I was known as a trailblazer, a woman who traveled in ways no one before me ever had. I was born in Tuscumbia, Alabama. When I was very young I contracted a severe disease. The disease caused me to lose my hearing and sight. For some time this caused me to live my life "at sea in a dense fog." Then, Anne Sullivan, a teacher from the Perkins Institute for the Blind, came to teach me how to communicate using other methods. It was a breakthrough when Anne helped me to associate the symbols for the word "water" on my hand as actual water was being poured over my other hand. I loved Anne for giving me this beautiful gift!

I was the first blind woman to earn a college degree. I wrote twelve books, including my autobiography, *The Story of My Life*. I also became a spokesperson for many causes and a champion for people with disabilities of all kinds. I died in 1968 at the age of 87.

Her Virtue

PERSEVERANCE

How many times have you tried something but failed miserably the first time? Or the second...or the third? Perseverance is the virtue of sticking with it—of trying again when you fail. Remember trying to learn how to ride a bike? Did you make it on the first try? Did you fall? If you fell, did you quit, never to try again? Chances are you picked yourself up (or had someone help you), wiped yourself off, and tried again. You know that old saying: if at first you don't succeed, try, try again!

Helen Keller is a model for perseverance. She was blind and deaf. She couldn't communicate. And with the help of Anne Sullivan, she tried and tried to learn the words needed to piece together a language. It didn't happen overnight. It didn't happen on the first try. She became upset at times. But through her perseverance, her ability to stick to it and keep trying, she was able to become a role model for future generations to do the same. Keep trying!

ACTIVITY

Helen Keller needed to learn a form of tactile sign language to communicate with those around her. Can you learn with Helen? Place the letter from the key underneath the signed letter and see what words of wisdom Helen is sharing with you.

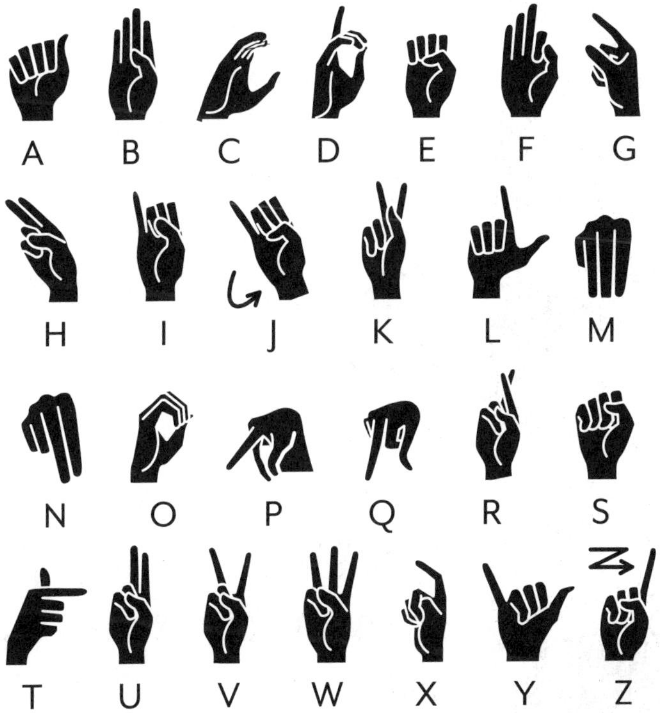

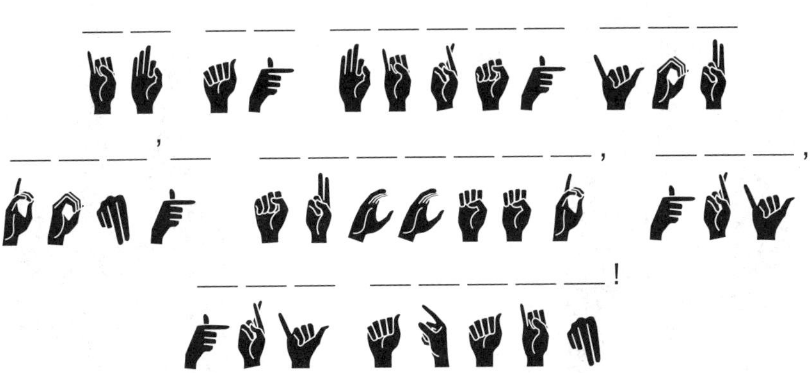

HER WORDS

The best and most beautiful things in the world cannot be seen or even touched—they must be felt with the heart.

The only thing worse than being blind is having sight but no vision.

We can do anything we want to if we stick to it long enough.

JOURNAL / REFLECTION

What did it feel like to succeed in something that you struggled with?

ACTION

Have a friend place a blindfold over your eyes. Without your friend's help, try to find your way around the room. Now try it again with the help of your friend.

Malala Yousafzai

Some people have said that If you look up the word "courage" in the dictionary, you might see a picture of me alongside the definition. Though that embarrasses me, that just might be true! I was born in Pakistan. At an early age I had become the face of human rights, and specifically education, in the face of very difficult living conditions. When I was eleven I wrote a blog that caught the attention of people around the world. Soon, television film crews were telling the story of my life.

In October 2012, I was shot in the face by terrorists while riding the bus home from school. The public attention that I received from around the world gave me international recognition. Following my recovery from the injuries, I became an outspoken advocate for children's education, especially for girls. At the age of 17, I received the Nobel Peace Prize in 2017. I graduated from high school in 2017 and am currently studying for a college degree at Oxford University in England.

Her Virtue

COURAGE

Have you seen the movie *The Wizard of Oz*? If not, check it out! In the movie, Dorothy, the main character, is a girl from Kansas who has a dream that she meets a scarecrow, a tin man, and a lion on her way to meet the Wizard of Oz. Each character is missing something: the scarecrow is missing a brain, and the tin man is missing a heart. But it is the lion who steals the show. He is missing something even more difficult to pinpoint or name—courage. He is afraid of everything and anything. Is there anything you are afraid of? Can you name it or is it difficult to do so?

Malala Yousafzai displays great courage. Where did that come from? Where did she get the courage to recover from the gunshot wounds she received from the terrorists? Probably like the lion in *The Wizard of Oz*, she received the courage to go on from somewhere deep inside of herself. Most people would say she received this courage, not from a wizard, but from God, the source of all courage.

ACTIVITY

Check the statements that are examples of courage

- ☐ **Trying a new food that you never tried before**
- ☐ **Trying a new ride at an amusement park**
- ☐ **Standing up for a person who is being bullied**
- ☐ **Completing a chore assigned by your parent**
- ☐ **Joining a classmate in the lunchroom who always sits by himself.**

JOURNAL / REFLECTION

Has trying something new been a challenge to you? Why?

ACTION

Choose one fear you have and pick one positive step in overcoming that fear.

HER WORDS

There are many problems, but I think there is a solution to all these problems; it's just one, and it's education.

I don't want to be remembered as the girl who was shot. I want to be remembered as the girl who stood up.

I speak not for myself but for those without voice...those who have fought for their rights... their right to live in peace, their right to be treated with dignity, their right to equality of opportunity, their right to be educated.